STORY: ISABELLE BOURNIER
DRAWINGS AND COLOURS: SÉBASTIEN CORBET

WILLIAM THE CONQUEROR
IN COMIC STRIP

Isabelle Bournier

Isabelle Bournier is a historian and author of several documentaries for young readers. She is also cultural and educational manager at the Mémorial de Caen.

Sébastien Corbet

Sébastien Corbet is an illustrator from Caen, born in 1972. After studying advertising, he turned to music. Concurrently, he paints and, after exhibiting for ten years, resumed his earlier passion for comic strip.

This book was published with support from the Conseil départemental du Calvados (Calvados Council).

Zone tertiaire de Nonant - 14400 BAYEUX
Tel.: +33(0)2 31 51 81 31 - Fax: +33(0)2 31 51 81 32
info@orepeditions.com - www.orepeditions.com

Editor: Grégory Pique - Editorial coordination: Sophie Lajoye
Layout: Sophie Youf - Graphic design: Éditions OREP
English translation: Heather Inglis
ISBN: 978-2-8151-0615-3 – © Éditions OREP 2023 - All rights reserved – Legal deposit: 2nd quarter 2022

French law n°49-956 dated 16 July 1949 on publications for young readers, modified by the law n°2011-525 dated 17 May 2011 – June 2022.

It all happened around the year one thousand, in 1035 to be precise. Robert, the duke of Normandy, was preparing to set off on a pilgrimage to Jerusalem. A long journey awaited him… Before leaving, he decided who would succeed him, should he never return home. He chose William, his young son…

JANUARY 1035 ROBERT, DUKE OF NORMANDY ARRIVES AT FÉCAMP CASTLE* WITH HIS SON WILLIAM.

LOOK WHO'S HERE! THE DUKE AND HIS BASTARD!

AND WHAT ROBERT IS ABOUT TO ANNOUNCE IS NOT GOING TO PLEASE EVERYONE.

THESE ARE THE MOST POWERFUL LORDS OF THE DUCHY...

TAKE MY ADVICE WILLIAM: BE ON YOUR GUARD!

SO YOU ARE HEADING FOR THE HOLY LAND** ROBERT. IT IS A LONG AND DANGEROUS JOURNEY.

WE WISH TO KNOW WHO WILL GOVERN THE DUCHY DURING YOUR ABSENCE.

MY SON IS STILL YOUNG, NOT EVEN 10 YEARS OLD, BUT SHOULD I NEVER RETURN HERE...

... HE SHALL SUCCEED ME.

YOUR SON WILL NEVER BE DUKE!

HE IS A BASTARD!

*AROUND THE YEAR 1000, FÉCAMP, ALONG WITH ROUEN AND BAYEUX, WAS ONE OF THE DUKES OF NORMANDY'S PLACES OF RESIDENCE.
**THE DUKES WERE GREAT BELIEVERS. THEY TRAVELLED TO JERUSALEM TO SEEK PARDON FOR THEIR SINS.

The oath of loyalty to William

THE DUCHY'S NOBLEMEN HAVE NO CHOICE BUT TO OBEY THEIR DUKE, AND SWEAR LOYALTY TO WILLIAM.

ROBERT! YOUR SON WILL SUCCEED YOU. WE SWEAR.

WE SWEAR.

WE SWEAR.

GILBERT DE BRIONNE* SWEARS AN OATH TO THE FUTURE DUKE.

YOU WILL DEFEND JUSTICE AND THE WEAK.

YOU WILL DEFEND JUSTICE AND THE WEAK.

RALPH DE GACÉ PRESENTS WILLIAM WITH A DAGGER.

YOU WILL FULFIL YOUR FEUDAL DUTIES.

*HE SWORE LOYALTY TO WILLIAM AND LATER BECAME ONE OF THE YOUNG DUKE'S GUARDIANS.

A plot against William

*GOLET WAS THE DUKE'S JESTER.

AVOIDING BAYEUX, HOME TO TOO MANY OF HIS ENEMIES, THE YOUNG DUKE GALLOPS AT FULL SPEED TOWARDS FALAISE.

AT DAWN, HE STOPS AT THE CASTLE IN RYES, WHERE HE IS WELCOMED BY HUBERT, A LOYAL LORD.

OPEN UP! I AM WILLIAM, YOUR DUKE!

BAM! BAM! BAM! BAM!

BUT?! WHAT BRINGS YOU HERE?

YOU TRAVEL ALONE? WITHOUT ESCORT?

I WOULD LOVE TO HAVE SEEN THOSE TRAITORS' FACES WHEN THEY REALISED THEY'D BEEN OUTDONE

MEANWHILE, MY SONS WILL ESCORT YOU TO FALAISE.

I AM GRATEFUL FOR YOUR ASSISTANCE, HUBERT...

... AND I THANK YOU FOR THE CLOTHES.

THE DUKE OF NORMANDY CAN'T TURN UP IN FALAISE JUST IN BREACHES*!!

*WILLIAM BARELY HAD THE TIME TO PUT HIS TUNIC ON OVER HIS TROUSERS.

*THE POPE'S PERMISSION WAS REQUIRED FOR ROYAL AND PRINCELY MARRIAGES.

Harold's visit...

*THE CITY OF CAEN.

*A PERSON WHO BETRAYS AN OATH.

At the Ladies' Abbey in Caen...

*Religious ceremony to devote a building to God. In this case, the Ladies' Abbey in Caen.

Preparation for the English expedition is underway…

The Battle of Hastings, 14 October 1066

William crowned king of England

England is covered in fortified castles

The great devastation*

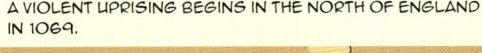

*Name given by the English to the last major military campaign led by William to conquer the north of England. Everything was pillaged, burned, massacred, during the winter. Many of those who survived finally perished from cold and hunger.

WILLIAM SHARES HIS TIME BETWEEN NORMANDY AND ENGLAND.

YOU LOOK UNSETTLED, WILLIAM.

HE IS DETERMINED TO EXTEND HIS ROYAL ESTATE* AND NOTHING WILL STOP HIM.

FOR HIM, YOU HAVE INDEED BECOME TOO POWERFUL.

PHILIP, THE KING OF FRANCE, HAS BECOME A THREAT TO THE DUCHY.

HE IS TRYING TO SOW DISCORD BETWEEN MY SON AND I...

...AND ROBERT HAS JOINED HIM.

YOUR SON'S ANGER IS NO LONGER ANY SECRET.

HIS IMPATIENCE TO BECOME DUKE OF NORMANDY HAS DRIVEN HIM TO TREASON!

SEEMS THE DUKE'S HEADIN' STRAIGHT BACK TO ENGLAND.

ALL THAT SCOT'S KING'S FAULT - BEEN WREAKING HAVOC AGAIN**!

SCOT WHO?

THE MONARCH FROM THE NORTHERN LANDS AS I UNDERSTAND...

CHATTER! CHATTER! BUT IS THE STEW NEARLY READY?

BECAUSE THE KING OF SCOTLAND IS NONE OF YOUR BUSINESS!

*FRANCE, AS WE KNOW IT TODAY, DIDN'T EXIST YET. THE KING'S ESTATE – WHICH HE WAS EAGER TO EXPAND – WAS STILL LIMITED.
**THE KING OF SCOTLAND HAD RESUMED PILLAGING IN THE NORTH OF ENGLAND.

Death of Matilda

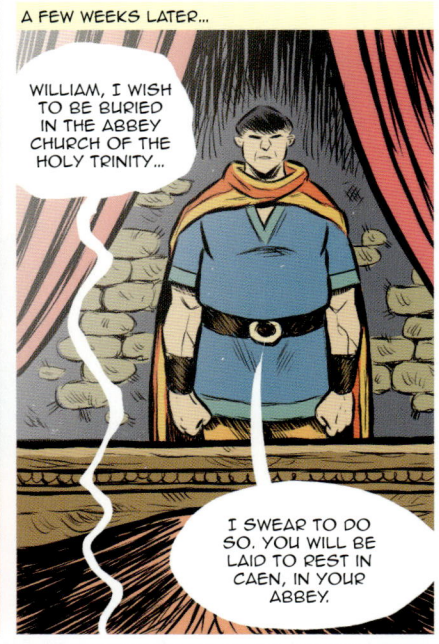

MATILDA FALLS ILL IN THE SUMMER OF 1083.

"THE DUKE HAS JUST ARRIVED. MAY I BECKON HIM?"

"YES, PLEASE DO."

"MATILDA, MY DARLING WIFE, YOU SEEM SO VERY WEAK."

"I AM TERRIBLY SICK AND NO REMEDY EASES MY PAIN."

A FEW WEEKS LATER...

"WILLIAM, I WISH TO BE BURIED IN THE ABBEY CHURCH OF THE HOLY TRINITY..."

"I SWEAR TO DO SO. YOU WILL BE LAID TO REST IN CAEN, IN YOUR ABBEY."

WILLIAM HEADS BACK TO ENGLAND THE FOLLOWING SPRING.

"THE SITUATION IS CAUSE FOR CONCERN MY LORD. UPRISINGS, MORE UPRISINGS..."

"AND WE ARE SHORT OF FUNDS TO PAY THE SOLDIERS."

ON THE CHRISTMAS OF 1085, WILLIAM GATHERS HIS COURT IN GLOUCESTER, ONE OF HIS ROYAL RESIDENCES.

"HAVE ALL THE KINGDOM'S NOBLEMEN ARRIVED?"

"THEY ARE ALL PRESENT! DESPITE THE SNOW, NONE OF THEM WOULD EVER MISS THE CHRISTMAS COURT."

"PERFECT! I HAVE AN ANNOUNCEMENT TO MAKE... LIKE NONE BEFORE!"

"ERR? NOT ANOTHER WINTER CAMPAIGN I HOPE?"

"... A COMPLETE INVENTORY* OF THE COUNTRY'S RICHES, COUNTY BY COUNTY."

"I WANT TO KNOW THEM ALL... TO LEVY NEW TAXES!"

*THE RESULTS OF THIS SURVEY (INCLUDING THE NAMES OF OWNERS AND THEIR RESPECTIVE PROPERTIES) ARE COMPILED IN TWO HUGE BOOKS REFERRED TO AS THE DOMESDAY BOOK.

The Domesday Book

THE KING'S SURVEYORS SET OFF ACROSS THE KINGDOM. THEY ARRIVE IN THE NORTH...

— WE'VE SCOURED ALL FOUR CORNERS OF THE COUNTY...
— YEP?! NOT MUCH LEFT AROUND HERE.

— GIVE ME YOUR NAME AND TELL US HOW MANY LIVE IN YOUR VILLAGE.
— M'NAME'S FINN. JUST THREE FAMILIES LEFT IN THE VILLAGE.

— THREE FAMILIES? WHERE'D THE OTHERS GO?
— WELL, THEY EITHER DIED OF HUNGER OR OF COLD, DURING THE WINTER REBELLIONS*.

— I'M SIWARD. I OWN ALL THE LAND IN THE VILLAGE...
— BUT I DON'T HAVE ENOUGH HANDS TO WORK ON IT.
— DEAD OVER THE WINTER OF 1069, I PRESUME...

— WE'LL NEVER BUILD ENOUGH MONASTERIES OR CATHEDRALS...
— ...FOR GOD TO ABSOLVE US OF THESE MASSACRES.

— YOU HAD NO CHOICE WILLIAM... YOU HAD TO QUELL ALL THE BARONS WHO REFUSED TO ACKNOWLEDGE YOU AS THEIR KING.

*DURING THE WINTER OF 1069-1070, WILLIAM'S ARMIES CRUSHED THE REBELLIONS THAT STRUCK NORTHERN ENGLAND. THIS WAS REFERRED TO AS THE HARRYING OF THE NORTH. DEPRIVED OF FOOD AND HEATING, HUNDREDS OF PEASANTS DIED OF HUNGER AND OF COLD.

William's death

BACK IN NORMANDY, WILLIAM HAS SET OFF TO WAGE WAR TO DEFEND THE FRONTIERS OF HIS DUCHY.

Burn the villages and the harvests! Spare nothing! The Duke's orders!

THE TOWN OF MANTES IS PILLAGED AND SET ON FIRE*.

Fire!

Fire, fire, everywhere!

William! Help! The Duke!

Argh!

WILLIAM IS TAKEN BACK TO ROUEN WHERE HE DIES A FEW WEEKS LATER, ON 9 SEPTEMBER 1087.

My son, I entrust you with England. I promised Normandy to Robert, and I will keep my word.

May God forgive him.

AFTER THE DUKE'S DEATH, WILLIAM'S BODY IS TAKEN TO CAEN. IT IS SWATHED IN A LEATHER SHROUD.

HE IS BURIED IN THE MEN'S ABBEY, IN THE MONASTERY HE FOUNDED.

*WILLIAM WENT TO MANTES TO FIGHT THE FRENCH KING PHILIP I AND HIS ARMY, WHO CONTINUED TO THREATEN THE NORMANDY BORDER.

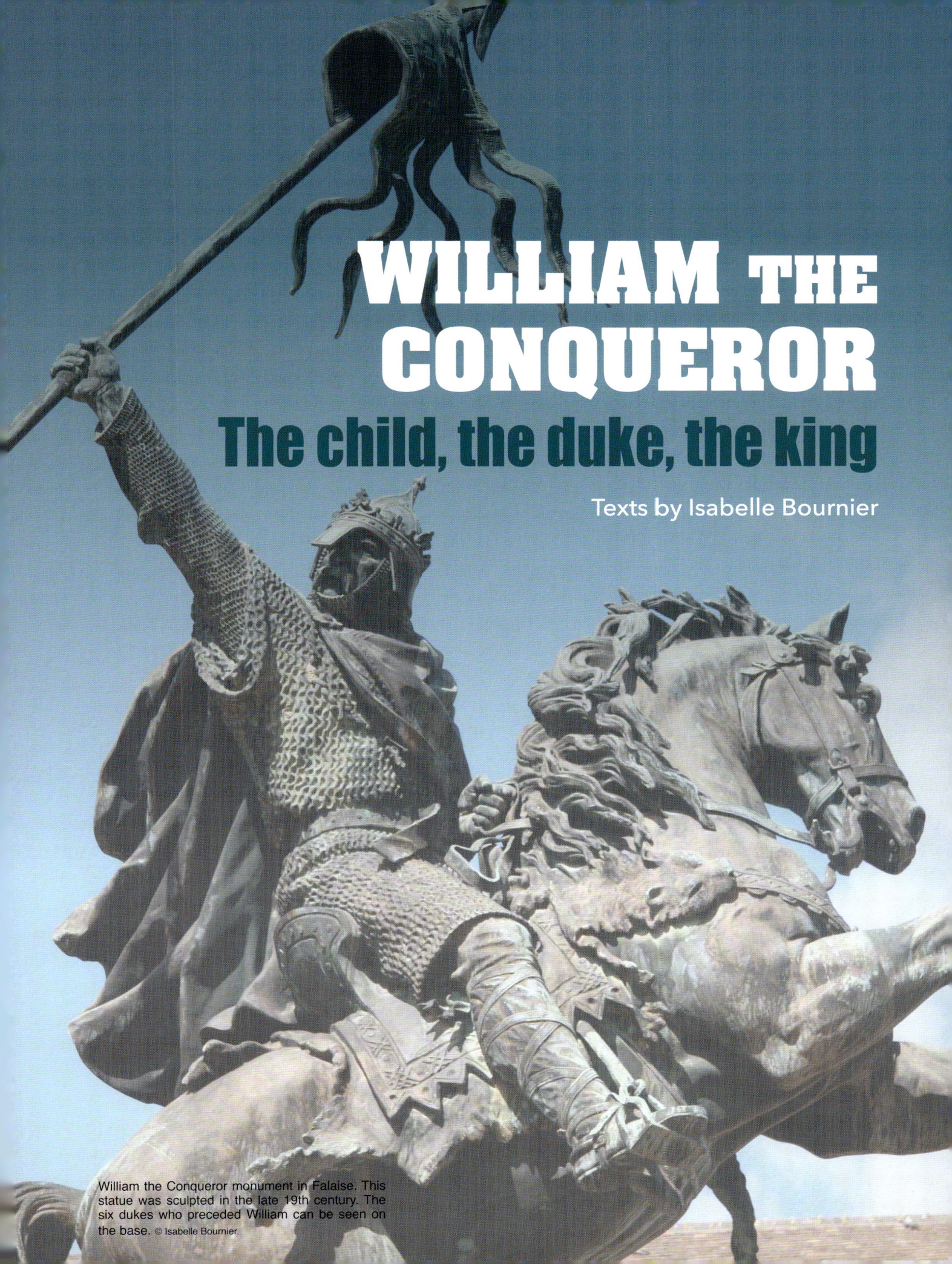

WILLIAM THE CONQUEROR
The child, the duke, the king

Texts by Isabelle Bournier

William the Conqueror monument in Falaise. This statue was sculpted in the late 19th century. The six dukes who preceded William can be seen on the base. © Isabelle Bournier.

WILLIAM'S LIFE IN 10 QUESTIONS

1/ Who were William's parents?

William was born in Falaise in 1027 or 1028. His father, Robert the Magnificent, was duke of Normandy. His mother, Herleva (also known as Arlette), is said to have been the daughter of a tanner and leather merchant. Since his parents were not married, William was nicknamed 'the Bastard'. William grew up in Falaise, probably at the castle with his mother. His father was often away.

Falaise Castle today From left to right, the large and small keeps and the high Talbot Tower. © Isabelle Bournier.

2/ What age was William when he became duke of Normandy?

Robert decided to set off for the Holy Land in 1035. He gathered together all the lords of his duchy in Fécamp, where he announced that his son, William, would succeed him. Robert died on his return home from the Holy Land. William became Duke of Normandy at the age of 8 years.

Statue of Robert the Magnificent, William's father. It is one of six statues representing the dukes of Normandy who reigned before William. © Creative Commons – Michael Shea, imars.

3/ Why was young William in danger?

After Robert's death, the lords of the land did not wish for William to be their duke and believed it was the right time to get rid of him. However, with help from his guardians who kept him in hiding, William managed to escape their wicked plots.

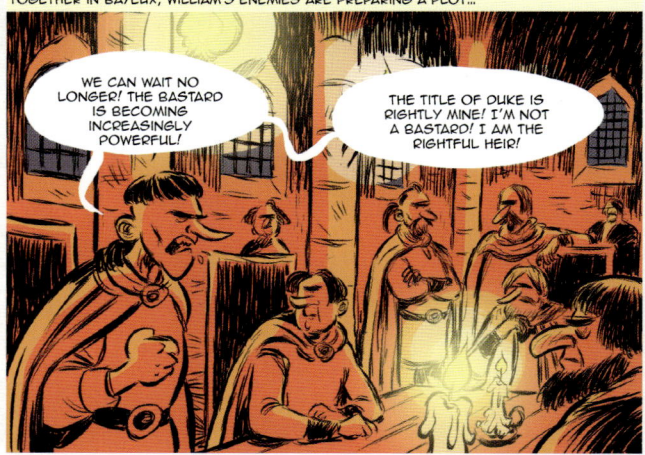

TOGETHER IN BAYEUX, WILLIAM'S ENEMIES ARE PREPARING A PLOT...

"WE CAN WAIT NO LONGER! THE BASTARD IS BECOMING INCREASINGLY POWERFUL!"

"THE TITLE OF DUKE IS RIGHTLY MINE! I'M NOT A BASTARD! I AM THE RIGHTFUL HEIR!"

4/ How did William get rid of his enemies?

At the age of 20, William decided to eliminate all those who had opposed him and wished him dead. With support from the King of France, he crushed his enemies at the Battle of Val-ès-Dunes, near Caen, in 1047. After this victory, William could finally rule over Normandy.

5/ How did William govern Normandy?

William restored order throughout the duchy, which he reorganised. He gathered a court reuniting the leading and most loyal lords. The court met in different towns on the occasion of key religious ceremonies (Christmas, Easter, Whit Sunday).

IN TURN, WILLIAM UTTERS HIS WAR CRY BEFORE LAUNCHING INTO BATTLE.

"DIEX AÏE !"

Scene of the Battle of Hastings depicting fighting between the English foot soldiers and two horsemen from William's army. © Detail of the Bayeux Tapestry - 11th century, photograph courtesy of Ville de Bayeux.

Portrait of William painted by a unknown artist in the 16th or 17th century. © National Portrait Gallery, London.

6/ What did William look like?

There is no portrait of William dating from the 11th century. However, we know he was tall for his time (1.73 metres/5 feet 8 inches), and of stocky build. William was a strict and very pious man. It seems that he could neither write nor speak English, but he was gifted in ruling over his duchy and leading his army to victory.

7/ Why was the Battle of Hastings so important?

At Hastings, William rid himself of his enemy Harold, who had been crowned King of England instead of William. Many English lords were killed during the battle. William replaced them with Normans. After Hastings, William was nicknamed, 'the Conqueror'.

8/ How did William succeed in taking control of England?

At first, William hoped the English would simply accept him as their king. However, they rebelled against him and William had to resort to force to crush them. The Normans were not in sufficient numbers to control the entire nation, so they built castles and monasteries to demonstrate who the new master of the land was.

9/ What became of England and Normandy after William?

Before he died, William shared his kingdom between his three sons. The eldest son, Robert, who was at loggerheads with his father, inherited Normandy. The second son, William Rufus, received the throne of England, and the youngest son, Henry, was given a large sum of money.

Henry, one of William's sons who later became king of England and duke of Normandy, after his brothers' deaths. In his hand, he is holding one of the abbeys he founded. © British Library.

10/ A short summary of William's life.

It's quite simple! His life can be divided into three periods, each one lasting around twenty years:
1027-1047: the duke's youth, a difficult period during which his life was threatened.
1047-1066: William was duke of Normandy.
1066-1087: William was duke of Normandy and king of England.

THE NORMAN HORSEMAN

William the Conqueror was an excellent warlord. He successfully formed a powerful and well-organised army which he led to victory several times. The typical Norman horseman benefited from excellent protective equipment, to play a leading role in the duke of Normandy's conquests.

- Helmet reinforced with iron bars
- Mail to protect the nape
- Spear
- The standard upon which William's army could be recognised
- Hauberk, or coat of mail, split in order to fold arms
- Nasal protection
- Wooden and leather shield
- Mace used to strike the enemy
- Shoes with crossed leather laces
- Spur
- Stirrup
- Sword

WHERE THE NORMANS LEFT THEIR MARK IN ENGLAND...

Today, many sites across England bear witness to the presence of the Normans. The most visible traces are in the form of castles, abbeys and cathedrals, the construction of which began shortly after William's Conquest of England. For example, Windsor Castle, a frequent place of residence of the British monarchy, dates back to that period. It has, of course, been extended since. The same applies to the famous Tower of London.

Cathedrals, abbeys and castles

The Normans had castles, cathedrals and monasteries built. They were similar to those in Normandy but much bigger. Their typical Romanesque architecture is referred to as Norman Style. It took dozens of years to build them and only a few, such as the Tower of London, were completed during William's life.

The Tower of London, made of Caen stone. The Tower can still be visited today. © Creative commons – Bob Collowân.

Caen stone

In Caen, William had a castle and two abbeys built, using Caen stone. After the Conquest, he had quantities of this stone taken to England, along with architect-monks. The stone was transported by boat. Many castles, cathedrals and monasteries are made of Caen stone. The Tower of London is the most famous.

Canterbury Cathedral is one of the oldest Christian churches in England. It was built by Lanfranc, the abbot who features in this comic strip. © Creative Commons – Hans Musil.

What about the British? Do they not speak a little Norman?

The Normans arrived in England with many words which were adopted in the English language. For example, the word *pocket* comes from the Norman *poquette*. A *mug* is called a *moque* in Norman. The Norman word *gardin* became *garden* in English. *Mei itou* translates as *me too*... Many English words that are used by the French are also of Norman origin (shopping, challenge, pickpocket, mug, etc.).

The word garden, seen here on a London signpost, actually comes from the old Norman word *gardin*. © Isabelle Bournier.

THE BAYEUX TAPESTRY

This incredible embroidery tells the story of the Conquest of England and offers a host information on 11th-century clothes, weapons and fortified castles. Here are a few scenes of this tapestry which you can visit in Bayeux.

A/ Harold has just told William that Edward, the king of England, has chosen William to succeed him to the throne.

Which character is William and which one is Harold?

B/ Upon Edward's death, Harold takes the throne instead of William.

What four objects were given to Harold on the occasion of his coronation?

C/ Preparations for the Conquest of England. What is going on in this scene?

D/ The Battle of Hastings was waged on 14 October 1066.

This scene depicts various weapons used by the combatants. Try to find them all.

Answers

Answers: A/ William is seated and Harold is standing in front of him. We can recognise him thanks to his moustache. They are in one of William's palaces, in Normandy. **B/** A globe, a crown, a sword and a sceptre. **C/** Carpenters have cut down trees and are building Viking longships. **D/** Spears, swords, axes and bows (lower border).

FÉCAMP

BAYEUX

CAEN

FALAISE

NORMANDY

IN WILLIAM'S FOOTSTEPS...

Falaise Castle

Caen Castle

The Men's Abbey and the Ladies' Abbey in Caen

Bayeux Cathedral

Fécamp Abbey

Test your knowledge

TRUE OR FALSE?

1/ Before the Conquest of England, William was nicknamed 'the Bastard'. Afterwards, they called him 'the Conqueror'.

2/ William and Matilda did not have permission to marry because they were cousins.

3/ William was king of Normandy and duke of England.

4/ Upon William's death, the duchy of Normandy and the kingdom of England were shared between his three sons and his six daughters.

FIND THE ODD ONE OUT!

Which of these objects does not belong to a typical Norman horseman?

NEED HELP?

QUIZ

1/ William was born in 1027 or 1028 and died in 1087. He lived in the: 10th century / 11th century / 12th century?

2/ After the Battle of Hastings, William became: king of England / duke of Normandy / king of France?

3/ When William was not in Normandy, who governed the duchy: his son Robert / his wife Matilda / his friend Lanfranc - Abbot of the Men's Abbey?

4/ William and Matilda had two vast abbeys built in Caen: Robert the Magnificent's Abbey and Herleva's Abbey (William's parents) / the West Abbey and the East Abbey / The Ladies' Abbey and the Men's Abbey?

Answers:

True or false: 1/ True. 2/ True. 3/ False. William was duke of Normandy and king of England. 4/ False, they were shared between his three surviving sons.
Find the odd one out: the leather boots, the boomerang and the rifle.
Quiz: 1/ 11th century. 2/ king of England. 3/ Matilda, his wife. 4/ The Ladies' Abbey and the Men's Abbey.